Anonymous

List of Ancient Monuments in the Rajshahi Division

Anonymous

List of Ancient Monuments in the Rajshahi Division

ISBN/EAN: 9783337385002

Printed in Europe, USA, Canada, Australia, Japan

Cover: Foto ©ninafisch / pixelio.de

More available books at **www.hansebooks.com**

Government of Bengal.

PUBLIC WORKS DEPARTMENT.

LIST OF ANCIENT MONUMENTS

IN THE

RAJSHAHI DIVISION.

Revised and corrected up to 31st August 1895.

PUBLISHED BY AUTHORITY.

Calcutta:

PRINTED AT THE BENGAL SECRETARIAT PRESS.

1896.

RÁJSHÁHI DIVISION.

CLASSIFI

[See Government of India, Home Department

I.—Those monuments which, from their present condition and historical or
II.—Those monuments which it is now only possible or desirable to save
the exclusion of water from the walls, and the like.
III.—Those monuments which, from their advanced stage of decay or

I. (a) and II (a).—Monuments in the possession or charge of Government
conservation.
I. (b) and II (b).—Monuments in the possession or charge of private

(1) RÁJSHÁHI

No.	District.	Locality.	Name of monument.	History or tradition regarding the monument.
1	2	3	4	5
1	Rájsháhi ...	Bágha ...	Mosque ...	Built about the year 1583A.D. This mosque was founded and is maintained out of an endowment of lands made by the Emperor Shahjehan.
2	Ditto ...	Kusumba, thána Manda.	Mosque of Sabar Khán.	It is said to be 300 years old, built by Sabar Khán, by birth a Bráhman, who became a Muhammadan. The tradition is that he was a zamindar, and when kept a prisoner at Murshidábád for some reason, he attracted the notice of the Begam by his singing. She interceded for him with the Nawab, who released the man and sent the Begam away with him, first allowing them to take away as much as they could help themselves to, from the Toshákhána in the space of one *prahar*, and with this the masjid was built.

(2) DINÁJPUR

				The Pál Kings, Buddhists, lived on the borders of Bográ and Dinájpur, and it is impossible to consider the antiquities of Dinájpur apart from those of Bográ. After the Pál Kings came the Sens, to whom are attributed the buildings from which the carved stones found in all parts of Dinájpur, Bográ and Máldá were taken.
3	Dinájpur ...	Chandera, Darail and Omaree.	Palaces (forts)	These remains of the palaces (forts) of the Pál dynasty are visible at Chandera, Darail and Omaree, and connected with them there are some curious stone remains at the shrine of Jogi Ghopi, corresponding with others preserved near thána Khytlál, in Bográ.

CATION.

Resolution No. 3—168—83, dated 26th November 1883.]

archæological value, ought to be maintained in permanent good repair.
from further decay by such minor measures as the eradication of vegetation,

comparative unimportance, it is impossible or unnecessary to preserve—

or in respect of which Government must undertake the cost of all measures of

bodies or individuals.

DISTRICT.

Custody or present use.	Present state of preservation and suggestions for conservation.	Classification.	REMARKS.
6	7	8	9
It is in the custody of Khondkar Tonsikul Islám, and is used as a mosque.	The mosque is kept in repair by the Khondkar from the proceeds of the lands given by the King of Delhi.	ii*b*	See page 36 of Hunter's Statistical Account of the Rájsháhi district.
Not in use	The place is in a ruinous state, but is worth repairing towards which the people residing in the neighbourhood are prepared to contribute.	iii	

DISTRICT.

Not in any particular custody	Ruins	iii.	

No.	District.	Locality.	Name of monument.	History or tradition regarding the monument.
1	2	3	4	5
4	Dinájpur ...	Meongabári, thána Patnítolá.	The Buddal pillar.	The following account of this pillar is taken from pages 131—141 of the Asiatick (sic.) Researches, Volume I. (London, 1806). An inscription on a pillar near Buddal. Translated from the Sanskrit by Charles Wilkins, Esq. Some time in the month of November in the year 1780, I discovered, in the vicinity of the town of Buddal, near which the company have a factory, and which at that time was under my charge, a decapitated monumental column which at a little distance has very much the appearance of the trunk of a cocoa-nut tree broken off in the middle. It stands in a swamp overgrown with weeds, near a small temple dedicated to Hara-Gouri, whose image it contains. Upon my getting close enough to the monument to examine it, I took its dimensions and made a drawing of it, and soon after a plate was engraved. It is formed of a single stone of a dirty grey complexion, and it has lost, by accident, a considerable part of its original height. I was told upon the spot that it had, in the course of time, sunk considerably in the ground, but upon my digging about the foundation, I found this was not the case. At a few feet above the ground is an inscription engraved in the stone, from which I took two reversed impressions with printer's ink. I have lately been so fortunate as to decipher the character, and I have the honour to lay before the Society a transcript of the original in the modern writing, and a translation, and at the same time to exhibit the two impressions I took from the stone itself. The original character of this inscription is very different from the modern form, but it so much resembles that on the plate found by Colonel Watson, at Monguoor, that I am induced to conclude it to be a work of the same period. The language is Sanskrit, and the whole is comprised in twenty-eight metrical verses of various measures. 14th July 1785. CHARLES WILKINS. PROSPERITY ! I.—Víra Dev was of the Sandilya race (a tribe of Bráhmans still extant) ; from him was descended Pañchál, of whose generation and of whom, was Garga born. II.—He another Sakra (Indra, the lord of the Heavens, who is supposed to be the Guardian of the East) was ruler, but of one quarter, and had no authority in other regions. He, too, was defeated by Duitya (evil spirits. Indra is said to have lost his kingdom for a while, to the Asuras or evil spirits) chiefs; but being a virtuous prince, he became supreme over every country without reserve, and his conduct was such that he laughed Vrihaspati (the tutor of the good spirits and the planet Jupiter) to scorn.

Custody or present use.	Present state of preservation and suggestions for conservation.	Classification.	Remarks.
6	7	8	9
There are two servants here, one a Bráhman who gets Rs. 7 a month, and another Hari on Rs. 3 a month. The former worships the god and the latter does miscellaneous work. These men are paid by zamindars Bhabání Prasád and Táriní Prasád Bhattáchárjya of Patiram.	The tank in which the pillar is situated is overgrown with aquatic plants. The pillar has been cracked; no one repairs it, and unless repairs are made soon, it will collapse. It is known by the name Bhím's stick. The zamindar will be called on to see that the pillar is looked after. ·	*ib.*	See article on pages 160—167 of Vol. II of Epigraphia Indica.

No.	District.	Locality.	Name of monument.	History or tradition regarding the monument.
1	2	3	4	5
				III.—Ichchhá (Love, Desire) was his wife; and, like love, she was the mistress of his heart. She was admired for the native purity of her mind, and her beauty was like the light of the moon. IV.—In his countenance, which was like the flower of the waters (the lotus), were to be traced the lines of four sciences (arms, music, mechanics, physics). The three worlds were held in subjection by his hereditary high rank. From these two was descended a Bráhman like Kamalayoni (Brahmá), and he took unto himself the name of Srí Darbha-páni. V.—Whose country, extending to Reva-Janak (perhaps the Nerbudda) to the father of Gourí (the snowy mountains that part India from Tartary-Gourí, one of the names of the Párvati, the consort of Siv), whose piles of rock reek with the juice exuding from the heads of intoxicated elephants, and whose snow-white mountains are brightened by the sun's rays; to the two oceans:—to that whence Aruna (the charioteer of the sun, the Aurora of the Hindus) riseth from its bed, and to that wherein the sun sinketh in the west, the Prince Srí Dev Pál (if this be the prince mentioned in the copper plate found by Colonel Watson, he reigned at Monghyr above 1800 years ago) by his policy, rendered tributary. VI.—At whose gates (although the prospect, hidden by the dust arising from the multitude of marching forces was rendered clear from the earth being watered by constant and abundant streams flowing from the heads of lustful elephants of various breeds), stood, scarce visible, amongst the vast concourse of nobles flocking to his standard from every quarter, Srí Dev Pál in expectation of his submission. VII.—Whose throne, that Prince (who was the image of Indra and the dust of whose feet was impressed with the diadems of sundry potentates), himself ascended with a flash of glory, although he had formerly been wont to offer him large sums of peetas (a square coin) bright as the lunar rays. VIII.—To him was born, of the Princess Sarkaré, the Bráhman Semsévar, who was like Som (the moon), the offspring of Atri, and a favourite of the most high. IX.—He adopted the manners of Dhanañjaya (one of the sons of Pándu, commonly called Arjun), and did not exult over the ignorant and ill-favoured. He spent his riches amongst the needy. He neither vainly accepted adulation, nor uttered honey words. His attendants were attached by his bounty, and because of his vast talents, which the whole universe could not equal, he was the wonder of all good men. X.—Anxious for a home and an asylum, he took the hand of Ranná (a princess of this name is also mentioned in Colonel Watson's plate), a Princess of his own likeness, according to the law, even as

DISTRICT—*continued.*

Custody or present use.	Present state of preservation and suggestions for conservation.	Classification.	REMARKS.
6	7	8	9

No.	District.	Locality.	Name of monument.	History or tradition regarding the monument.
1	2	3	4	5
				Siv, the hand of Siva (Sivá is the feminine of Siv)—even as Hari the hand of Lakshmí.

XI. From this pair proceeded into life, bursting forth like Guha (a name of Kártik) with a countenance of a golden hue, the fortunate Kedára Miśra, whose actions rendered him the favourite of heaven. The lofty diadem, which he had attained, shone with faultless splendour, kissing the vast circumference of the earth. His extensive power was hard to be limited, and he was renowned for boundless knowledge raised from his own internal source.

XII.—The ocean of the four sciences, which had been at a single draught drunk up, he brought forth again, and laughed at the power of Agastya (who is said to have drunk up the ocean).

XIII.—Trusting to his wisdom, the King of Gour (the Kingdom of Gour anciently included all the countries which now form the kingdom of Bengal on this side the Brahmaputra, except Monghyr) for a long time enjoyed the country of the eradicated race of Utkal (Orissa) of the Hoons (Huns) of humbled pride, of the kings of Drávir (a country to the south of the Carnátic) and Gurját (Goozerat), whose glory was reduced, and the universal sea-girt throne.

XIV.—He considered his own acquired wealth the property of the needy, and his mind made no distinction between the friend and the foe. He was both afraid and ashamed of those offences, which condemn the soul to sink again into the ocean of mortal birth: and he despised the pleasures of this life, because he delighted in a suprame abode.

XV.—To him, emblem of Vrihaspati (the preceptor of the good spirits, and the planet Jupiter) and to his religious rites, the prince Srí Súra Pál (who was a second Indra, and whose soldiers were fond of wounds) went repeatedly; and that long and happy companion of the world, which is girt with several oceans as with a belt, was wont, with a soul purified at the fountain of faith, and his head humbly bowed down, to bear pure water before him.

XVI.—Vanwá, of celestial birth, was his consort, with whom neither the fickle Lakshmí, nor Satí (the consort of Siv) constant to her lord, were to be compared.

XVII.—She, like another Devakí (the real mother of Krishna), bore unto him a son of high renown, who resembled the adopted of Yaśodá (the foster mother of Krishna) and husband of Lakshmí. (Rukminee, the consort of Krishna. She is here called Lakshmí, in compliance with the idea of her being a descent of that goddess.)

XVIII.—This youth, by name Sree Gourava Miśra, was acquainted with all the constellations. He resembled Rám, the son of Jámadagni (this is neither the conqueror of Ceylon nor the brother of Krishna). He was another Rám.

DISTRICT—*continued*.

Custody or present use.	Present state of preservation and suggestions for conservation.	Classification.	REMARKS.
6	7	8	9

No.	District.	Locality.	Name of monument.	History or tradition regarding the monument.
1	2	3	4	5

XIX.—His abilities were so great, that he was solicitous to discover the essence of things, wherefore he was greatly respected by the Prince Srí Náráyan Pál. What other honour was necessary?

XX.—His policy (who was of no mean capacity, and of a reputation not to be conceived), following the sense of the Veds, was of boundless splendour, and, as it were, a descent of Dharma, the Genius of Justice. It was regulated by the example of those who trust in the power of speech over things future, who stand upon the connation of family, who are in the exercise of paying due praise to the virtues of great men, and who believe in the purity of astrology.

XXI.—In him was united a lovely pair, Lakshmí and Sarasvatí, the Disposer of Fortune and the Goddess of Science, who seemed to have forsaken their natural enmity, and to stand together pointing at friendship.

XXII.—He laughed to scorn him who, in the assemblies of the learned, was intoxicated with the love of argument, and confounded him with profound and elegant discourses framed according to the doctrine of the Sástras; and he spared not the man who, because of his boundless power and riches, was overwhelmed with the pride of victory over his enemy in the field.

XXIII.—He had a womb, but it obstinately bore him no fruit. One like him can have no great relish for the enjoyments of life! He never was blessed with that Giver of Delight, by obtaining which a man goeth unto another almoner (he had no issue to perform the srádh for the release of his soul from the bonds of sin. By *another almoner* is meant the Deity).

XXIV.—He who was, as it were, another Válmíki (the first poet of the Hindus, and supposed author of the Rámáyan), born in this dark age of impiety amongst a dreadful and a cruel race of mortals, was a devout man, who displayed the learning of the Veds in books of moral tales.

XXV.—His profound and pleasing language, like Gangá, flowing in a triple course (he is supposed to have written in three languages), and constant stream, purifieth and delighteth.

XXVI.—He, to whom and to those of whose generation, men were wont to resort as it were to Brahmá, waited so long in expectation of being a father, that at length he himself arrived at the state of a child.

XXVII.—By him was recorded hereupon this lasting column, the superior beauty of whose shaft catcheth the eye of the beholder, whose aspiring height is as boundless as his own ideas, which is, as it were, a stake planted in the breast of Kali (time), and on whose top sits Tárkshya (otherwise called Garur), the foe of serpents and favourite bird of Hari, the line of his own descent.

DISTRICT—continued.

Custody or present use.	Present state of preservation and suggestions for conservation.	Classification.	REMARKS.
6	7	8	9

No	District.	Locality.	Name of monument.	History or tradition regarding the monument.
1	2	8	4	5
				XXVIII.—Garur, like his fame, having wandered to the extremity of the world, and descended even unto its foundation, was exalted here with a serpent in his mouth. This work was executed by the artist Vindu Bhadra. The local people of the present day cannot tell by whom the pillar was constructed. Close to the pillar there is a *Mandir* in which statues of Siva and goddess Gouri are worshipped.
5	Dinájpur ...	One at Gopálganj 4 miles north of Dinájpur, and another at Chehalghazi, on the banks of the Púrnabhaba, one mile south of Dinájpur.	The Giants' tombs.	Traces of the Buddhist Kings are left in the Giants' tombs, as well as in the tank of Mahípál Dighí. The tombs are 50 or 60 feet long, and represent Buddha entering into the state of *Nirvàn* ; but they have been appropriated by the Muhammadans, and are worshipped as belonging to Muhammadan pirs. One of them, 57 feet long, at Gopálganj, four miles north of Dinájpur, is called ' Pír-i-chehel Ghazi,' and there is another a mile south of Dinájpur, on the banks of the Púrnabhaba. A small fair is held annually on the last Mohurrum day at Chehelghazi.
6	Ditto ...	Hamtabad ...	The mosque and tomb of Pír Bazar-ruddin.	The mosque, situated close to the tomb, is a fine one with two inscriptions still standing, and there are a number of Hindu carved pillars and stones about. The neighbourhood is full of brickwork, and it has been ascertained that these remains are those of the ancient Hindu city of Mahasu, whence the pargana takes its name. There is a mound near, called Takht-i-Husain Shah, which appears to be the remains of a Buddhist stúpa. There are several other mounds which have not yet been explored. The Muhammadans certainly used portions of Hindu buildings to build their own mosques, and excavation might throw light on the legends of Maheś Rájá, preserved by Dr. Buchanan-Hamilton.
7	Ditto ...	Gañgárámpur ...	Bán Garh (Fort) Tomb of Sultan Shah.	The ruins of Bán Garh occupy the east bank of the Púrnabhaba, of which the quadrangular citadel, 1,800 feet by 1,500, is surrounded by a high rampart of bricks, and on the south and the east by a ditch and on its west face is a large projecting part, probably the outworks of a gate. In the centre there is a large heap of bricks, said to have been the Rájá's house, and on the east face is a gate, and a causeway about 200 feet long, leading across the ditch into the city, which has been square, of above a mile in diameter, and has also been surrounded by a rampart of brick, and by a ditch. Towards its south-east corner is the tomb of Sultán Shah, which contains many pillars and an entrance of the Hindu period. Near it are two celebrated pools, called

DISTRICT—*continued.*

Custody or present use.	Present state of preservation and suggestions for conservation.	Classification.	REMARKS.
6	7	8	9
Has no custodian ...	Exploration very desirable ...	ii*a*	
Ditto ...	The tomb of the Pír is very much neglected and badly requires repairs, but the Collector does not recommend expenditure on the part of Government for its repairs. The mosque is in a state of very good preservation.	iii	See page 635 of Vol. II of Martin's Eastern India.
Ditto ...	In ruins, cannot be rebuilt or maintained.	iii	See pages 659 to 665 of Vol. II of Martin's Eastern India, and for sketch of entrance door and a pillar of Sultan Shah's monument, see page 662 of the same volume. See pages 95 to 100 of Vol. XV of the Archæological Survey Reports in regard to the antiquities at Gaṅgárámpur and Devikot.

No.	District.	Locality.	Name of monument.	History or tradition regarding the monument.
1	2	3	4	5
				Amrita and Jivat. On the north-east corner of the city is a large heap of bricks, said to have been the ruins of a temple of Mahádeva, whom Bán rájáh worshipped here. There are other ruins in the neighbourhood and on the other side of the Bráhmaṇí. Bán Garh supplied materials to builders of Gaur and to the Rájás of Dinájpur.
8	Dinájpur ...	Gangárámpur ...	Mosque and Tomb of Mulla Atta-uddin Shah.	There are numerous inscriptions on the mosque and on the tomb, and they are said to date from the end of the 14th or the 15th century. A fair is held annually here, called the Dahaldighí melá, and the tomb (at which a lamp is still kept burning) is much frequented as a place of worship.
			Dhole Dighí (Tank).	Attached to it is a tank called Dhole Dighí with its gháts composed of a flight of stone stairs.
9	Ditto ...	Devíkot or Dumduma.	Tombs of Pír Havakhari and Pír Bahaudin.	There are here three tanks and the shrines of two saints named Pír Havakhari and Pír Bahaudin. At one of these shrines there are four inscriptions, one of Kaiksus Shah, the earliest in Bengal. These deserve to be preserved.
10	Ditto ...	Devíkot ...	Tapan Dighí, Dohal Dighí and Kala Dighí.	Seven miles south from Dumduma is the largest Dighí in the district, called Tapan, 4,700 feet by 1,750, which was dug by Rájá Bán, the Asur. East of this tank is Khardaha, where he fought with Krishna. Dohal Dighí is another tank, 4,000 feet by 1,000 feet, on the high banks of which are some ruins, which are evidently of the Hindu period. The carved stones were brought here from Bánnagar. Kála Dighí is another tank said to have been dug by Kalaráṇí, the spouse of Bán Rájá; it is 4,000 feet by 800 feet.
11	Ditto ...	Ekdala ...	Fort ruins ...	This was a Muhammadan fort, where Ghyasuddin Shah and Sikandar Shah successively defied the power of Feroz Shah, the Delhi Emperor, and which Hussain Shah afterwards turned into his royal residence. It is situated on the east bank of the Chiramati, west of Támbuli. The place is covered with jungle; but, as there is a shrine, it is believed there may be inscriptions somewhere about. The royal residence, probably that of Hussain Shah, the Kasaba and the Baherhata, or outer enclosure, have been traced here. A tank running north and south, much older than the Muhammadan ones, shows that it occupies an old Hindu site, Dhanjor, whence the pargana takes its name.
12	Ditto ...	Gorághát ...	Tomb of Ismail Ghazi.	The remains of a very large frontier post and the tomb of Ismail Ghazi, a leader of the time of Barbak Shah are found here.
13	Ditto ...	Atrai ...	Tomb of Mahí Santosh.	There are several tombs and shrines on the Atrai. The most noteworthy is that called Mahí Santosh, with two inscriptions of Barbak Shah.

DISTRICT—*continued.*

Custody or present use.	Present state of preservation and suggestions for conservation.	Classification.	REMARKS.
6	7	8	9
In use and in the custody of Abid Hossain Fakir of Rájíbpur.	The walls of the Durgah are breaking down and are overgrown with trees. The ghát is also going to ruins.	ii*b.*	
Has no custodian ...	Conservation and exploration very desirable. Copies of inscriptions should be sent to the Government Epigraphist.	ii*a.*	
......	......	ii*b*	See pages 659 to 661 of Vol. II of Martin's Eastern India.
Has no custodian ...	Some fine tanks, the remains of a brick fort, and traces of many brick buildings still exist. Exploration needed.	iii.	
Ditto	Exploration needed; but the Collector does not recommend any expenditure for the preservation of the tomb.	iii	
Ditto	Exploration needed and inscriptions should be sent to the Government Epigraphist. Tomb not worth preserving.	iii	

No.	District.	Locality.	Name of monument.	History or tradition regarding the monument.
1	2	3	4	5
14	Dinájpur ...	Gopálganj ...	Mosque ...	This is very ancient, and has on it an inscription of Barbak Shah, A.D. 1365.
15	Ditto ...	Ditto ...	Temples of Prán Gopál and Rás Mohan.	There are two temples at Gopálganj, one with 5 and the other with 25 spires. Both these temples were built by Mahárájá Rám Náth Roy, Báhádur, the smaller one in 1743 A.D. and the larger one in 1754 A.D. He placed the image of Prán Gopál (from whom the place derived its name) in the former and that of Ras Mohanji in the latter. The place gradually became depopulated and overgrown with jungle until the growing inconvenience of worshipping the idols there came to be so keenly felt, that the idols were removed to the Mahárájá's own house at Dinájpur, where they now are. The temple and some of its spires were struck by lightning three times, and having, as stated above, ceased to be a place of worship, has now become almost a ruin.
				The temple with twenty-five spires is a beautiful and noble specimen of old architecture. Mr. Robinson, a former Collector of Dinájpur, proposed in 1873 to arrange for the repair and preservation of it, but the estimated cost (about Rs. 1,30,000) being prohibitive, the idea was abandoned. As the temples are no longer required as places of worship, the Mahárájá has no objection to Government undertaking the task of their conservation.
				The temple at Yogighopa is the most elegant of all temples in the district of Dinajpur. The image is placed on the small altar seen through the door, and is covered by a dome. Although the building is of a considerable size and cost an immense sum (it is said 20,000l.), there is no apartment in it above 12 feet, and the stair is steep, perfectly dark, and will not admit a man to walk with both shoulders equally advanced.
16	Ditto ...	Kántanagar ...	Temple of Kánta.	The building of this temple was commenced in 1704 A.D. by Mahárájá Prán Náth Roy, Báhádur, and completed in 1722 A.D. by his son, Mahárájá Rám Náth Roy, Báhádur. Mahárájá Rám Náth Roy, on his way back from Delhi, where he went on a visit to the Emperor, visited Brindában, the holiest city of the Vaishnabs, and was so charmed with the beautiful image of Gobindji at that place that he resolved to possess and remove it to Dinájpur by means fair or foul. The god Govindji appeared before him in a dream, and while advising him to desist from a sacrilegious design on his person, offered him the means of getting possession of an equally beautiful image.

DISTRICT—*continued.*

Custody or present use.	Present state of preservation and suggestions for conservation.	Classification.	REMARKS.
6	7	8	9
Has no custodian ...	Considered well worth preserving.	ii*a*	
Formerly in the custody of the Mahárájá of Dinájpur, but now abandoned since the idol has been removed to his own house.	In ruins. Cannot be rebuilt or maintained.	iii	See pages 626 and 627 Vol. II of Martin's Eastern India. A drawing of the temple before its partial demolition will be found as the frontispiece of volume II.
In use and in the custody of the Mahárájá of Dinájpur. It is used for the worship of the idol.	The temple is in good repair and looked after by the family of the Mahárájá of Dinájpur.	ii*b*	See pages 628 and 629 of Vol. II of Martin's Eastern India.

No.	District.	Locality.	Name of monument.	History or tradition regarding the monument.
1	2	3	4	5
				The temple was thoroughly repaired about three-quarters of a century ago by the late Maháráni, when a portion of it was struck down by lightning. It is now in very good condition. The temple is used in locating Kántají and in worshipping him.
				The place is considered very holy, and is visited by large crowds of Vaishnabs, particularly those belonging to the Srí Samprdáya. The temple is in good repair and looked after by the Mahárájá. It stands on the ruins of a fort that is said to have belonged to Virát Rájá of Mahabhárat renown. The place where he kept his herds of cattle is known as Uttar Gogriha, now surrounded by the mounds of four ramparts and three intermediate ditches. There are several mounds inside. The other ruin is at Sonka, about 4 miles East of Buganj on the Atraye River.
17	Dinájpur ...	Govindanagar or Thákurgrám.	Temple of Govinda.	Was built by Mahárájá Rám Náth Roy, Báhádur, who dedicated it to the worship of Govindjí. The Garh and other adjoining buildings were built by him when the place was one of his favourite residences.
				The temple is an ordinary pucca building which is now reduced to ruins requiring repairs badly. God Gobindjee, for whose accommodation this temple was built, has been removed to a straw-built house. There is a channel excavated from the temple to the Dinájpur Rájbari for the purpose of conveying the god from there to Dinájpur. This channel is known by the name of Rándará. The temple is of no architectural value and does not demand preservation.
18	Ditto ...	Pírganj ...	Fort of Mahádeva. Mogalankot fort.	On the west of the Tangan river and near the southern extremity of the district are extensive ruins of a brick fort among which is a carved stone. Mahádeva is said to have been a contemporary with Virát Rájá. There is another ruined fort close by, known as Mogalankot.
19	Ditto ...	Birampur ...	Garh Pigulai (fort.)	These remains were excavated to get bricks for the Northern Bengal State Railway. A fort, with a brick rampart, called Garh Pigulai, must have been a place of some strength. Perhaps this, and the earthen forts near the Jamuná, may have had something to do with the Kakshal revolt in Akbar's time.
20	Ditto ...	Jagadal ...	Residences of Secundar Shah and Mayarudra.	Secundar Shah built his favourite villa at Secundra on the Tangan, and Hossein Shah formed a fine road from this river to Punshhoga; it is said to have been 348 cubits wide, with a large ditch and many fine trees on each side and bridges constructed of bricks. In the centre of the island between the two rivers are a tank and ruins of the abode of Mayarudra, who was contemporary with Virát.

DISTRICT—*continued.*

Custody or present use.	Present state of preservation and suggestions for conservation.	Classifi-cation.	REMARKS.
6	7	8	9
Of no use now ...	This building is almost a ruin. It is now surrounded by dense jungle.	ii*b*	See pages 629 and 630 of Vol. II of Martin's Eastern India.
......	......	ii*b*	See page 632 of Vol. II of Martin's Eastern India.
Has no custodian ...	......	iii	
......	......	ii*b*	See pages 642-643 of Vol. II of Martin's Eastern India.

No.	District.	Locality.	Name of monument.	History or tradition regarding monument.
1	2	3	4	5
21	Dinájpur ...	Dhíbar ...	Pillar ...	It is a beautiful stone monolith in the middle of a big tank which is one mile square.
22	Ditto ...	Kutivari ...	Tanks called Melan Dighi, Gor Dighi, and Alta Dighi. Tomb of Pír Budal Dewan.	About 1¼ miles west from the Baliya is a very large tank called Melan Dighi, beyond which are Gor Dighi, and Alta Dighi; between the latter two are extensive ruins of bricks called Barn háta, of which the thick walls and a small chamber can still be traced. The fort had double walls and an intermediate ditch, where is a tomb of Pír Budal Dewan.
23	Ditto ...	Mahípur ...	Mahípál Dighí (tank).	This is a large tank extending 3,800 feet from north to south and 1,100 feet from east to west, excavated by Rájá Mahípál of the Pál dynasty. There are several ruins of bricks and stones close by and at Bangaon.
24	Ditto ...	Khyetlal ...	Palace (fort) of Vali Rájá.	East of the temple of Siddheswarí are the ruins of Vali Rájá's house and of a large town, which contains many heaps of bricks, traces of walls and roads. In the neighbourhood are some stone images, cut asunder by Kálápáhár.
25	Ditto ...	Sitákund near Nawabganj.	Sitákund (tank).	It has brick ruins with a cavity in the centre, where Sítá, the Queen of Rama of Ajodhyá, lived in her exile; and the hermitage of Válmiki, the author of the *Rámáyana*, was on the banks of the Karatoyá; he used to bathe at the Tarpan Ghát, which is now held sacred.
26	Ditto ...	Virátgarh near Ghoraghát.	Virátgarh (fort).	Here are the ruins of a square fort protected by a ditch about 60 feet wide. It contains many heaps of bricks which are small and very rudely formed. On the west was the gate. Here it is believed by the people that Virát Rájá had his palace.
27	Ditto ...	Satparagarh near Ghoraghat.	Satparagarh (fort).	Within the fort and on a high mouldering bank of the river, is a heap of bricks, called the King of Bengal's throne, which appears to have been a structure of about 100 feet in diameter, supported by small arches. The piers are very thick, containing within them many masses of carved stone, evidently taken from anterior buildings.
28	Ditto ...	Jogighopa in Bodalgáchi.	Temple of Mahádeva.	The shrine, where the image is placed, resembles a tomb, and is sunk below the level of the ground.
29	Ditto ...	Atapar in Lálbasar.	Palace (fort) of Ushopál. Temple of Haragauri.	On the Tulsi and near the tomb of Nimay Shah are ruins in bricks and stones, among which are a capital of a pillar with four tigers' heads and a brick at the tomb with a human figure. They are ascribed to Ushopál, whose palace was here. West of this is another ruin, said to have been the house of Mahípál, south of which is a small square rampart, and a ditch; near it is the temple of Haragauri, which has a pillar. On it is an inscription.

DISTRICT—*continued*.

Custody or present use.	Present state of preservation and suggestions for conservation.	Classification.	REMARKS.
6	7	8	9
In no one's custody, but within the zamindari of Koch Kurila zamindars.	The pillar is in good order but the tank is silting up.	iib	
....	......	...	See page 640 of Vol. II of Martin's Eastern India.
. ...	... .	...	See pages 634 to 636; also page 641, and Plate No. II of Vol. II of Martin's Eastern India.
......	.. ...	...	See pages 683-684 of Vol. II of Martin's Eastern India.
......	......	...	See page 678 of Vol. II of Martin's Eastern India.
......	......	...	See pages 679 to 680 of above Vol.
......	......	...	See page 681 of above Vol.
......	......	...	See page 668 of Vol. II of Martin's Eastern India, where a sketch of the temple is given.
......	......	...	See Vol. I of the Asiatic Researches. Also pages 671-672 of Vol. II of Martin's Eastern India.

No.	District.	Locality.	Name of monument.	History or tradition regarding the monument.
1	2	3	4	5
30	Dinájpur ...	Virátpat, tháná Howara.	Palace (fort) of Virát Rájá.	Howara was on the frontier of Matzyadesa, where Rájá Virát is said to have stationed a considerable part of his army. A ruinous fort and mounds are still there. Madan is another ancient place near the above, where the General of the Rajah resided and where there is a fort and other ruins, as also old tanks.
31	Ditto ...	Kichak, tháná Howara.	Fort ...	About 4½ miles north from the Tháná, are the ruins of a fort and town, which are said to have belonged to Kichak. On the north are the mounds called Draupadidhá and Raghunáthpur. The latter has a rather interesting statue of Buddha, worshipped as Raghunáth. It is supported by the Yoni of a linga. About three-quarters of a mile beyond the fort, and near Karatoyá, are the remains of a town, where was the house of the female donor of Kichaka, which is said to have been covered with enamelled tiles. Here Rájá Háváchandra and his minister Gaváchandra, the two fools of the local tradition, are said to have lived the first at Gopináthpur and the second at Vagdvár.

| 32 | Jalpaiguri... | Jalpesh in Maynagari, Western Duars. | Temple of Siva | This is the most conspicuous ruin in the district. It is a large square building constructed of very durable bricks. The temple is on a mound surrounded by a moat, and is near the bank of the river Jhardan. The floor of the basement is sunk some depth in the mound, and a flight of steps leads down to it, while above rises a large square building surmounted by a dome, round the base and top of which run galleries. The height from basement floor to top of dome is about 92 feet; the lower storey is 78 feet square, and the upper stories are 38 and 36 feet square respectively. The dome is 34 feet outer and 26 feet inner diameter, and 17 feet in height. The building has little or nothing of architectural beauty. The object of worship in this temple is a "Siva Linga," which is fixed in a hole in the floor of the underground basement, and has no "Gauripat." The depth of the floor below the surface causes it to be at all times more or less covered with water, and it is customary to bale this out before the idol is worshipped. The earliest tradition of this Siva is that it was placed where it now stands, or somewhere in the vicinity by a King of Assam, named Jalposvar. After a lapse of time it appears to have been overlooked or its existence forgotten, and the following is the legend connected with its re-discovery and the erection of the Jalpes temple. |

DISTRICT—concluded.

Custody or present use.	Present state of preservation and suggestions for conservation.	Classification.	REMARKS.
6	7	8	9
......	......		See pages 674-676 of Vol. II of Martin's Eastern India.
......	......		See above and Plate V.

DISTRICT.

No custodian ...	In ruins, but it should be preserved.	iii	

No.	District.	Locality.	Name of monument.	History or tradition regarding the monument.
1	2	3	4	5
				Some 300 years ago, Prán Náráyaṇ, Rájá of Kuch Bihár, dreamt that Śiva appeared to him and said that he was at Gortali, and would be found if effective search were made. Inspired by this dream, Prán Náráyaṇ left his usual place of residence and, accompanied by an army and many attendants, went and commenced the search, starting at Gortali. After a long search, and with the aid of a cow which, it was found, used every day to go to the neighbouring jungle and drop its milk, the Rájá succeeded in tracing the Śiva Linga, on which he ordered the erection of a temple over the spot. The present temple was then commenced. The Rájá and his son having died, the temple was finally completed by his grandson, Mahendra Náráyaṇ.
33	Jalpaiguri...	Purbadeber (about one and a half miles east of Jalpeś.)	Temple of Śiva	This is a smaller red brick temple about a mile and a half east of Jalpeś, and ascribed to the Rájá who built Jalpeś. The main entrance to this building is of massive stone.
34	Ditto ...	Ditto ...	Temple of Peṭ-káṭi Devi.	This is situated a little north of Mynagarí. The idol, which stands there still, had ten hands ; of these, three hands, also the stomach and nose, have been cut off, hence the idol is known as the Petkati Thákuráṇí. Tradition says that this idol was originally called Bhadreśvarí, but that, being mutilated by Kálápábar, it got the name of Peṭkáṭi Devi. It is not known who erected the temple.
35	Ditto ...	Bhitargarh, par-ganá Baikanṭha-pur.	Bhitargarh ..	This is the largest fort and must have been a very large and strong fortification in old days, being no less than 4½ miles in length by 2 or 2½ in breadth. The fort is surrounded by several moats, there being on one side no less than six, and there is in it a large tank with the remains of ten gháts, at each of which traces of red bricks are seen. Little is known of the origin of this garh, but it is generally believed to have been built by one Prithvi Rájá, of a dynasty long prior to the Kuch Bihár one.
			Prithvisul Díghí tank.	The tank is called ' Prithví-sul Díghí,' and it is said that the Raja of that name jumped into it and was drowned to avoid being touched by the Kichaks, who had then invaded his country. The water of this tank is wonderfully pure and clear, and free from weeds ; it is but little used, in consequence of a local superstition against drinking it.
				The city is supposed to have consisted of four separate enclosures, the innermost being the Rájá's palace. It must have been a place of great strength, in spite of its large size. The Talma Nadí, on the west, was utilised to fill one of the moats.

DISTRICT—*continued.*

Custody or present use.	Present state of preservation and suggestions for conservation.	Classification.	REMARKS.
6	6	8	9
.. ...	Full details desirable ...	iii	
,.....	Ditto ...	iii.	
... ..	There are no visible ruins, but the mounds near which old bricks are to be found are probably the remains of the old buildings. Exploration necessary.	iii.	

d

No.	District.	Locality.	Name of monument.	History or tradition regarding the monument.
1	2	3	4	5
36	Jalpaiguri...	Boda ...	Thákuráṇi Bhitargarh.	The next garh in size is that in Boda, called the Thákuráṇi Bhitargarh. This is an enclosure about a mile square, surrounded by very wide triple moats. It is supposed to be co-eval with the larger Bhitargarh.
37	Ditto ...	Jalpaiguri ...	Baikunṭhapur Garh.	The smallest garh is that of Baikanṭhapur, at Jalpaiguri, on the river Kalla, known as the Rájbári. This has for some time been the residence of the Raikuts of Baikanṭhapur. It is surrounded on three sides by double moats, and on the fourth the Kalla river flows by. It is not supposed to date much further back than 180 years. There are the ruins of a fine brick building here but it can be of no great age.

Nil.

38	Rangpur ...	Pirganj ...	Hatibandha Mosque.	Said to have been erected some 500 years ago by Shah Ismail.
39	Ditto ...	Ditto ...	Tomb of Jogul Bokhari.	It is the shrine of Jogul Bokhari, a holy man, and is used for the same purposes as other shrines. Pilgrims repair to it for spiritual benefit.
40	Ditto ...	Ditto ...	Tomb of Pír Ismail Gazi.	This monument of Pír Ismail Gazi is known as the *Baradargá*. It is situated six miles north of Pirganj police-station. Its history or tradition is not known, nor can it be ascertained by whom and when it was erected. It is a very old monument.
41	Ditto ...	Kata Dowar, pargana Khás Táluk.	Mosque of Shah Ismail.	Said to have been erected some 500 years ago by Shah Ismail.

DISTRICT—*concluded.*

Custody or present use.	Present state of preservation and suggestions for conservation.	Classification.	Remarks.
6	7	8	9
......	Exploration necessary ...	iii.	
	Ditto ...	iii.	

DISTRICT.

DISTRICT.

There are some lákhraj lands appertaining to it which are enjoyed by Akbar Hossain for the custody of it.	......	iib	
Wahid Buksh is the custodian of it. The Bog family of Islampur, of which Buharuddin and Fusaiuddin are two principal members, enjoy considerable quantity of lákhraj lands for the custody of the shrine.	No steps have hitherto been taken to repair it. Exploration needed. Conservation desirable.	iib	
In the custody of Banki Miah, Kedár Ullah Miah, and others.	In good condition. Banki Miah, Kedár Ullah Miah, and the others duly repair and take great care of it.	iib	
......	......	...	

No.	District.	Locality.	Name of monument.	History or tradition regarding the monument.
1	2	3	4	5
42	Rañgpur ...	Kasba ...	Mausoleum of Shah Jalal Bokhari.	This is said to have been built some 400 years ago by one Shah Jalal Bokhari.
43	Ditto ...	Dimla ...	Fort of Dharma Pál Rájá.	About two miles south of the great bend in the Tistá are the remains of a fortified city, said to have been built by Dharma Pál Rájá. It is in the form of a parallelogram, about a mile from north to south, and half a mile from east to west. The defences consist of a high rampart of earth, which at the south-east corner is irregular, and retires back to leave a space, that is much elevated, and is said to have been the house of the Rájá's minister (Dewan-kháná). A ditch about 40 feet wide surrounds the town except on the east. In the centre of each of these three faces, is a gate, defended by outworks, and in these are a good many heaps of bricks. There were square bastions on each side. The earth from the ditch was thrown outwards and forms a slope. At a distance of about 160 yards from the ditch on the north-east and south sides, are parallel ramparts and ditches, which enclose an outer city, where the lower populace is said to have resided. Beyond these on the south is another enclosure, in which the horses were kept. Dharma Pál, whose troops occupied this city, used to live about three-quarters of a mile distant, where are several tanks and heaps of bricks; this place is now known as Baramolla Tara-kazi, where 25 pious Moslems assemble to whom it is dedicated. On the banks of the Hangrighosha, north from the ruins of the Rájá's house is seen the place where he disappeared in a battle against Mayanavati, his sister-in-law, whose residence on the west bank of the Deonai river, about two miles west from the fort of Dharma Pál, was built on the same plan with that of her brother-in-law, only the inner city has been a square of about 400 yards each side. It is surrounded by an outer rampart at about 100 yards from the ditch.
				At a considerable distance south from this, was a circular mound of earth, called Hariśchandrapál, about 40 feet in diameter in which a stone building was discovered. Hariśchandra's daughter was married to Gopichandra, the son of Mayanavati, who succeeded his uncle Dharma Pál.
				Two and a half miles north-west of Dimla is a small ruined fort, called Goriberkoth; and near Várupí is another, known as Rámergarh, said to have been built by a certain Ráma, a servant of the Vihár Rájá. It is nearly circular, about a quarter of a mile in diameter and consists of an earthen rampart and ditch, which are drawn in an irregular zigzag form.

DISTRICT—*continued.*

Custody or present use.	Present state of preservation and suggestions for conservation.	Classification.	REMARKS.
6	7	8	9
......	Exploration needed ...	iii	
......	......	iii	See pages 449 to 452 and two sketches and plate No. IV of Vol. III of Martin's Eastern India. See page 312 of Hunter's Statistical Account of the Rangpur district.

No.	District.	Locality.	Name of monument.	History or tradition regarding the monument.
1	2	3	4	5
44	Bañgpur	Jolpis	Fort of Prithu Rájá.	It is ascribed to Prithu Rájá, and consists of four consecutive enclosures. The innermost is said to have been the abode of the Rájá, being a parallelogram of about 600 yards from north to south, by half as much from east to west; but at the north end a small portion is cut off from its east side, by an earthen rampart in order to secure the place from any attack that might be made from a large tank, that is adjacent. The defence of the other parts has been a brick wall. The large tank adjacent to the citadel is about 800 yards from north to south and 700 from east to west. It has five ghâts, paved with bricks. The inner city, which surrounds the citadel and the tank, is about 1,930 yards from east to west and 345 from north to south. It had a brick rampart and a ditch, which are still traceable. The middle city extends about 3,530 yards from east to west and 6,350 from north to south; but its north face, where the rivulet enters its ditch, is strengthened by an additional rampart. Near its southern end is a tank, called Baghpukhori, where the Rájá kept some tigers; and in the northern area there are two small heaps of bricks, which are supposed to be the ruins of the house of the minister. In both the inner and middle cities there have been subdivisions separated by ramparts and ditches, both running parallel to the chief defences of the place, and cutting the former at right angles. The outer city is surrounded by a low rampart and ditch and is supposed to have been occupied by the lowest of the populace, on which account it is called Harirgarh. It extends 300 yards from the western rampart and 570 yards from the southern rampart of the middle city. The total length of the outer part, from north to south, is six miles.
45	Ditto	Mouthanakot, thâná Dhap.	Fort ruins	A small earthen fort which is attributed to the Kings of Komatapur. Dháp or Dhale-Rájya was the kingdom of Háva or Bhava Chandra, whose stupidity is known throughout Bengal.
46	Ditto	Bhootmári	Road	Rájá Nílámbar, the last of the Hindu dynasty, constructed a fine road, which extends from Komatapur to Ghoraghát, Dháp, Malanga, Pírganj, and Vagdvar. Where the country is low it is raised to a very great height, and is a grand work, worthy of a magnificent prince.
47	Ditto	Komatapur, near Lálbazar.	Fort	Komata was the capital of Rájá Nílambar, which the Moslems besieged. Their camping ground is represented by large mounds, serving as redoubts on the bend of the rivulet, their back being protected by a strong rampart of earth and a wide ditch.

DISTRICT—*continued.*

Custody or present use.	Present state of preservation and suggestions for conservation.	Classification.	REMARKS.
6	7	8	9
.. ...	......	iii	See pages 443 to 446 and sketch plan of fort, &c., in Vol. III of Martin's Eastern India. See page 311 of Hunter Statistical Account of the Rangpur district.
......	......	iii	See page 424, of Vol. III of Martin's Eastern India.
......	......	ib	See page 425 of Vol. III of above work.
......	......	iib	See pages 426—438 and Plates I, II, and III of Vol. III of Martin's Eastern India. See page 314 of Hunter's Statistical Account of the Rangpur district.

No.	District.	Locality.	Name of monument.	History or tradition regarding the monument.
1	2	8	4	5
				The city is of an oblong form and about 20 miles in circumference, of which about five were defended by the river Dhorla. The remainder was fortified by an immense bank of earth, and by a double ditch. The earth from the inner ditch seems to have formed the rampart, and, that from the outer was thrown towards the country, so as to form a kind of glacis. The rampart is about 130 feet in breadth at the base and from 20 to 30 feet in perpendicular height. The outer ditch is about 250 feet wide. There were four gates on the sides. On the road leading from the big ruin in the centre towards the south to Ghoraghat, large quantities of debris exist, which shows that the principal buildings were here, extending for about three miles. Though local tradition ascribes these ruins to the Moguls, yet the pillars and other relics give evidence of anterior and Hindu work. The gates had outer works to protect them; they are known as Síladvár, Vagdvár, and Hokodvár. Near the last, is the fortress, where the *Pátra* or the minister resided; it is about a mile square. North of it, and at Sítaláváts, is a large mass of grey granite, hollowed out in the form of a rude goblet; it is said to be the King's bath. Its sides are six inches thick; the diameter is 6½ feet, and the cavity is 3½ feet deep; and there is a sort of step inside. Within the town the chief object of interest is the *Pát* or the palace, which is quadrangular, and has a ditch, about 60 feet wide. It is about 1,880 feet from north to south and 1,860 from East to West. Within the brick wall of the inner enclosure the most striking object is a large mound, about 360 feet square at the top and about 30 feet high; it was faced with bricks. There are some tanks and two wells about ten feet in diameter, which are lined with bricks, which went down to about 20 feet below the outside ground level. Here was also the temple of Komatesvari, now represented by a small square heap. Other mounds represent the Rájá's palace. Scattered about the place, are several relics of stone, of which many are carved with figures; and among the pillars one was 22 cubits in length, but only two and-a-half cubits in circumference. The rather modern temple of Komatesvari was built by Prágnáráyan, the fourth Rájá of Vihár, in A. D., 1665, the original goddess being recovered by him from the rivulet Singimári, which was said to have been the fortunate amulet of Bhaga-datta.
48	Rañgpur ...	Malanga ..	Fort ...	About four miles south of the thana, is a line of fortification, which crosses the great road, that leads from Komatapur to Ghoraghát, and is attributed to Rájá Nilambar. The line extends about two miles east and one mile west, and seems to

DISTRICT—*continued*.

Custody or present use.	Present state of preservation and suggestions for conservation.	Classification.	Remarks.
6	7	8	9
......	......	iii	See pages 455 and 456 of Vol. III of Martin's Eastern India.

No.	District.	Locality.	Name of monument.	History or tradition regarding the monument.
1	2	3	4	5
				have been an outwork to another set of lines, that connect the Karatoyá and Ghoraghat. These lines consist of a rampart of earth thrown up from a ditch, about 40 feet wide. These works were constructed by Upendra, tenth Rájá of Vihár, in order to check the progress of the Moslems, whose territory Ismail Gasi had advanced thus far to the north.
49	Rangpur ...	Vagdvár ...	Residence of Rájá Bhavachandra.	These ruins are attributed to Bhava Chandra Rájá, whose residence was here. Here were roads paved with bricks, disposed in a tesselated form. About four miles west of this is the site of the temple
			Temple of Vagiswari.	of Vágiśvarí, whose statue exists, and who was the family deity of Bhava Chandra.
50	Ditto ...	Palargarh ...	Fort of Pala, the last Pál Rájá.	These ruins are attributed to the last prince (Pál Rájá) of the Dhápréjás, who lived here.
51	Ditto ...	Lorapat ...	Fort (palace) of the Lora Rájá.	Lorapat is about three and-a-half miles south-west from Pirganj. Here are some ruins attributed to Lora Rájá, a relative of Bhavachandra. This house seems to have occupied a space included within a brick wall, and was provided with two tanks. A little east from his house are three heaps of bricks, of which one is called the hall for entertaining strangers and another his office for transacting business.

No.	District.	Locality.	Name of monument.	History or tradition regarding the monument.
52	Bográ ...	Sherpur and Dhar Makum.	Tombs of Ghazi Tarkun Shahid.	These shrines (tombs) are two in number, one, situated in the town of Sherpur, is known as Sir Makum, the other at a place called Dhar Makum. The former is said to contain the head and the latter the trunk of Tarkun Shahid, a Ghazi, slain in battle by a Hindu Rájá who lived in a place called Rájbári-Mukunda, 4 miles south-west of Sherpur. The Hindu Rájá referred to above, was King Ballal Sen.
53	Ditto ...	Mahásthán Garh	Fort ruins ...	This is the most important relic of antiquity to be met with in the district. The account given of it in Hunter's Statistical Account of Bogra (pp. 192, et seq.) is full of myths and fables. In ancient Sanskrit literature it is known as Síla Dvípa. The river Karatoyá divided itself into two branches near the place, uniting again about a mile north of the present town of Bogra. This place may have been called Dvípa for this reason: but Buddhistic stúpas are called in this district by the vulgar as Dháp, and sometimes as Dvíp. Síla, again, seems to be a slight change of the Buddhistic word Síla (morality). Sila Dvípa or Sílá Dvípa was

DISTRICT—*concluded*.

Custody or present use.	Present state of preservation and suggestions for conservation.	Classifi-cation.	REMARKS.
6	7	8	9
...··	...···	iii	See page 456 of Vol. III of Martin's Eastern India. See pages 312 and 313 of Hunter's Statistical Account of the Rangpur district.
...···	····..	iii	See page 457 of Vol. III of Martin's Eastern India.
...·,·	...···	iii	See pages 457 and 458 of Vol. III of Martin's Eastern India.

DISTRICT.

Custody or present use.	Present state of preservation and suggestions for conservation.	Classifi-cation.	REMARKS.
There are some fakirs who guard the shrines. People make pilgrimages to them.	The shrine at Sherpur is still in a state of good preservation, while the one at Dhar Makum is now completely in ruins.	ii*b*	See page 190 of Hunter's Statistical Account of the Bogra district.
The mosque is in charge of Matwallis.	The Muhammadan mosque is kept in good preservation by the Matwallis. The ramparts of the fort, which grew up after the Muhammadan occupation of the place, are also in good preservation.	ii*b*	See page 192, *et seq.* of Hunter's Statistical Account of the Bogra district.

No.	District.	Locality.	Name of monument.	History or tradition regarding the monument.
1	2	3	4	5
				undoubtedly a sacred place of the Buddhists. The north-east angle of the fort was described by the local people as *Dvíper koṇ* (the Dvipa corner). The name is striking as on reaching the angle the remains of a *stúpa* are seen beyond the ramparts on the riverside, on the top of which a Vaishnaba mendicant has established himself. The people point out three other *drípa* (as they call them) all on the eastern side, just above the bed of the Karatoyá, the present Muhammadan mosque occupying the site of the southernmost *stúpa*. It is thus perfectly clear that what is called Mahásthán was originally a group of Buddhistic stúpas on the bank of the Karatoyá river, and the whole place obtained the name Sila Dvípa or Silá Dvípa under the later Hindu Kings of the Sena dynasty, who favoured the worship of Siva and Krishna in preference to Buddha. Two famous temples were built, one sacred to Skanda and the other to Govinda, and emblems of Siva were set up all about the place. No vestiges of the temples of Skanda and Govinda remain, but their sites are still well known, and from the two points on the north and the south, between which alone the stream of the Karatoyá is peculiarly sacred, and where the bathing of the Náráyaṇí Yoga takes place. The southernmost of the four stúpas appears to have been converted into a Sivite temple, and it was this temple which was destroyed and desecrated by the Muhammadans and replaced by a mosque, the broken emblem of the god Siva is still lying at the place.

The Muhammadan mosque is now in charge of Matwallis and is kept in good preservation. The ramparts of the fort, which grew up after the Muhammadan occupation of the place (which must have followed closely on the conquest of Bengal by Bukhtiyar Khiliji) are also in good preservation. The legends that are now related are utterly unworthy of belief, and the Síla Deví of these legends is only an imaginary being, whom ignorance has substituted for Síla Dvípa.

Parasurám is said by local tradition to have ruled here over 22 princes; he was killed by a Muhammadan saint, Shah Sultan Huzrat Aulinya. Sítá was exiled here by Rama of Ajodhyá. Vali the Asura King, is also believed by the people to have reigned here. He was succeeded by his son Bána Virát who was the next King of Matsya-desá. |
| 54 | Bográ ... | Virat (in the Jaipur Government estate) | Palace of Virat | It has been believed that somewhere in the vicinity of these estates lay the capital of the great prehistoric Hindu Rájá Virát who figures prominently in the story of the Mahábhárat. That this popular belief is not without foundation is evident from the fact that at a place called Virát, about 16 miles off from Khañjanpur an annual fair meets under the |

DISTRICT—*continued.*

Custody or present use.	Present state of preservation and suggestions for conservation.	Classification.	REMARKS.
6	7	8	9
......	......	iii	

No.	District.	Locality.	Name of monument.	History or tradition regarding the monument.
1	2	3	4	5
				name of " Virát-melá," and broken remains of an ancient house which seems to have taken ages to be reduced to its present state, are still pointed out as once forming a part of the palace of Virat. This single fact has thrown a veil of historic mystery over this place. If it is admitted that these remains were really once the palace of Rájá Virát, it may very reasonably be concluded that these Government estates, being so near to the supposed palace of such a powerful Rájá, enjoyed no small share of his wealth and prosperity. Piles of bricks, evidently remains of ancient buildings, seen here and there in jungly tracts of land, long forsaken by men, suggest that ages back this place was once inhabited by a rich and influential people. In some cases bricks, reduced to dust by the work of ages, are found scattered over a great distance and bear testimony to the unfathomable antiquity of the buildings of which they must have once formed a part. In the eyes of an antiquarian these things cannot but attach great interest to this place. But mouldering as they have been from age to age, it is impossible to find out anything of archæological value in these remains.
55	Bográ ...	Belamla, (in the Jaipur Government estate.)	Temples ...	There are other cases, however, where the buildings were constructed quite in recent times, and so they remain almost whole and entire. At Belamla, a village nearly two miles from Khañjaopur there is a group of twelve temples built by the local merchant-zamindars and said to be a century and-a-half old. They form a square with a small yard in the middle, and have an emblem of the deity Siv in each of them. There is scarcely anything remarkable in these temples, beyond that they are very strongly built, as testified by the fact of their being only very slightly damaged by the influence of time. It is believed that the *Chotta Nadi* which runs over a distance of about 10 miles between the Tulsí Gañgá and Jamuná was excavated by these merchants. It still retains the name of " Káṭá Jamuna."
56	Ditto ...	Ditto (ditto) ...	D o l m a n c h a temple.	A few decaying nice little buildings within the compounds of the house of the local lady zamindar, Drobmayí Choudhurání are more worthy of notice. They are less old than the temples of Belamla, having been constructed only about a century ago, but in point of workmanship the biggest of them, the Dolmañcha, is far superior to the latter. Indeed, in this respect it may be said to be superior to many proud edifices of the country. This building affords us some opportunity of judging the skill of the old race of native masons. What commands the visitor's notice most in this building is that various financial figures, congenial, perhaps, only to the Oriental taste, have been skillfully wrought on its walls.

DISTRICT—*continued*.

Custody or present use.	Present state of preservation and suggestions for conservation.	Classification.	REMARKS.
6	7	8	9
......	......	...	For a reference to Belamla see page 197 of Hunter's Statistical Account of the Bogra district.
......	......	iii	

No.	District.	Locality.	Name of monument.	History or tradition regarding the monument.
1	2	3	4	5
57	Bográ ...	Rághabpur (in the Jaipur Government estate.)	Remains of temples.	At Rághabpur, a village about two miles north of this place, there are remains of a few small temples whose antiquity nobody can fathom. From their appearance these temples seem to have been of exceptionally strong construction. The outward plaster and parts of the bricks under it have been worn out, but the structures still seem to defy decay and ruin.
58	Ditto ...	Sikola (ditto) ...	Tank ...	The old tank in the mansa Sikola, only lately repaired has a far greater interest attached to it than any of the above structures Referring to this pond old residents of the locality say, that a rumour had been handed down to them by their forefathers to the effect that there was a temple somewhere within it. This pond, it should be noticed here, is perhaps the oldest one in these estates. This story was all along disregarded and discredited as groundless. But traces have, the other day, been discovered of the existence of something like a small building under the surface of the water. It has not been examined but the coolies who worked on the tank got upon its top and showed that it occupies a space of about three square yards and has a gate on its eastern side. About 9 feet of the water was baled out in order to permit of the removal of the mud that had accumulated on the four sides of the tank. The water in the centre is still about four feet deep, but that on the roof of the supposed temple is only a cubit deep. It is unfortunate that the outlay of more money (Rs. 1,600 have been expended on this work in two years) is necessary to make a full discovery of this object of curiosity. The coolies would not dare to pass through the little gate while it is still under water. It would be highly interesting to pump out the remaining volume of water and examine the temple, as also its contents. To the antiquarian this would be a matter of great interest. A masonry ghát on the southern side of the tank made of exceptionally good bricks has also been dug out.

DISTRICT—*concluded.*

Custody or present use.	Present state of preservation and suggestions for conservation.	Classification.	REMARKS.
6	7	8	9
......	......	iii	

DISTRICT.

No.	District.	Locality.	Name of monument.	History or tradition regarding the monument.
1	2	3	4	5

Nil.

STATE.

Custody or present use.	Present state of preservation and suggestions for conservation.	Classification.	REMARKS.
6	7	8	9

Geographical Index to Ancient Monuments.

RAJSHAHI DIVISION.

Index of Ancient Monuments by Classes.

Classification of Building.	District.	Village.	Page.
1	2	3	4
Forts			
Baikunthapur Garh	Dinájpur	Atápur	20
Ban Garh (Fort)	Jalpaiguri	Jalpaiguri	26
Bhitargarh	Dinájpur	Gangárámpur	12
	Jalpaiguri	Bhitargarh	24
	Dinájpur	Chandera	2
	Ditto	Darail	2
	Rangpur	Dimla	28
	Dinájpur	Ekdala	14
Garh Pigulai	Ditto	Birámpur	18
	Rangpur	Joipia	80
	Dinájpur	Khyrtial	20
	Ditto	Kiobak	22
	Rangpur	Komatapur	80
Mahadéva's	Dinájpur	Pirgánj	18
Mahásthán Garh	Bográ	Mahásthán Garh	34
	Rangpur	Malañga	82
Mogalankot	Dinájpur	Pirgánj	18
	Rangpur	Mouthanakot	80
	Dinájpur	Omaree	2
Pálargarh	Rangpur	Pálargarh	34
Sátpárágarh	Dinájpur	Sátpárágarh	20
Thákurási Bhitargarh	Jalpaiguri	Bodá	26
Virátgarh	Dinájpur	Virátgarh	20
Viratpat	Ditto	Virátpat	22
Mansoleums Shah Jalal Bokhari's	Rangpur	Kasba	28
Mosques	Rájsháhi	Baghá	2
	Dinájpur	Gopálgánj	16
Hátibandha	Rangpur	Pirganj	26
Mulla Attauddin Shah's	Dinájpur	Gangárámpur	14
Pir Bazarruddin's	Ditto	Hemtabad	11
Sabar Khan's	Rájsháhi	Kusumba	2
Shah Ismail's	Rangpur	Kata Dowár	26
Palaces Lorapat	Ditto	Lorapat	24
Virát	Bográ	Virát (in the Jaipur Government Estate).	36
Pillars Baddal	Dinájpur	Meongabári	4
	Ditto	Dhibar	20
Residences Bhava Chandra's	Rangpur	Vágdvár	34
Mayarudra	Dinájpur	Jagadal	18
Socundar Shah's	Ditto	Ditto	18
Roads	Rangpur	Bhootmári	80
Tanks Alta Dighi	Dinájpur	Kativari	20
Dobai Dighi	Ditto	Devikot	14
Dhole Dighi	Ditto	Gangárámpur	14
Gor Dighi	Ditto	Kutivari	20
Kála Dighi	Ditto	Devikot	11
Mahipál Dighi	Ditto	Mahipur	20
Melan Dighi	Ditto	Kutivari	20
Prithvisul Dighi	Jalpaigari	Bhitargarh	24
	Bográ	Sikola (in the Jaipur Government Estate).	40
Sitákund	Dinájpur	Sitákund	20
Temples Tapan Dighi	Ditto	Devikot	14
	Bográ	Belamla (in the Jaipur Government Estate).	38
Dolmancha	Do.	Belamla (in the Jaipur Government Estate).	38
Govinda	Dinájpur	Govindanagar	18
Haragauri	Ditto	Atápur	20
Kánta	Ditto	Kántanagar	16
Mahádeva	Ditto	Jogighopa	20
Parbati Devi	Jalpaigari	Purbadebar	24
Prán Gopál	Dinájpur	Gopálganj	16
	Bográ	Rághaipur (in the Jaipur Government Estate).	40
Rás Mohan	Dinájpur	Gopalganj	16
Siva	Jalpaigari	Jalpesh	28
Do.	Ditto	Purbadebá	24
Vagiswari	Rangpur	Vágdvár	34
Tombs Ghazi Tarkan Shahid's	Bográ	Dhar Makum	34
Ditto	Do.	Sherpur	36

www.ingramcontent.com/pod-product-compliance
Lightning Source LLC
Chambersburg PA
CBHW032116080426
42733CB00008B/964